Dedicated to Savy and Peanut, who make every day an adventure. Thank you for traveling the world with us.

IRELAND

Educational Resources, Crafts & Activities for Kids

Sarah M. Prowant, MSN-Ed, RN

Savy Activities
Colorado, USA

Savy Activities© All Rights Reserved

TERMS & CONDITIONS

This product is licensed for single use only (single home or classroom). Redistributing, selling, editing or sharing any part of this product in any part thereof is strictly forbidden without the written permission of Savy Activities. You may make copies for your personal use but will need to purchase separate licenses for use in additional classrooms and/or schools. Failure to comply is a legal copyright infringement and will be prosecuted to the full extent of the law.

When posting photos of any part of this product on social media, please give credit to "Savy Activities" by hyperlinking to our website and tagging us as @SavyActivities on social media.

We reserve the right to change this policy at any time. If you have any questions regarding this or other of our materials, please contact us directly.

FOR BEST RESULTS:

 When assembling a 3D model, glue a second piece of thick paper with a craft glue stick to back of each sheet of model pieces (prior to cutting pieces) to provide additional stability when assembled.

 Laminate all cards & posters with at least 3 ml lamination for additional protection.

 If printing from an ebook, cardstock paper (>60 lbs) provides best results for cards, models and manipulative activities, while standard printer paper is adequate for recipes, lessons, etc. Please set printer to "FIT TO PAGE" when printing for best results.

FOLLOW US ON SOCIAL MEDIA!

 @savyactivities

 /SavyActivities

www.SavyActivities.com

WHATS INCLUDED:

- Ireland Poster, Flag, & Landmarks
- Landmark & Country Pinning
- Ireland Counties Poster
- Ireland Fun Facts Cards
- Ireland History Timeline Poster
- St. Patrick's Cathedral Model
- St. Patrick and the Lost Lamb Mini-book
- Celtic Knot Activity
- Celtic Symbol Tracing
- Celtic Harp Craft
- Gaelic Alphabet Cards
- Potato Stamping Activity
- Grow a Potato Activity
- Types of Potatoes Life-Size Flashcards
- Soda Bread Recipe
- Colored Candy Rainbow Experiment
- Rainbow Popsicles Activity
- Irish Step-Dancing
- Leprechaun Photo Props
- Pot 'O Gold Counting
- Leprechaun Maze
- Green Nature Hunt
- Punnett Squares Genetics Activity
- Claddagh Card Craft
- Melted Straw Shamrock Craft
- Shamrock Blessings Cards
- Shamrock Life Cycle, Anatomy & Tracing
- Game of Rings
- Irish Blessing Cards
- Ireland Fauna 3-Part Cards
- Temperate Deciduous Forest Matching & Trophic Layer Cards
- Ireland Currency - Euro
- Titanic Model & Shipwreck Site Pinning
- Irish Language Cards

Ireland

National Flora: Shamrock
National Fauna: Irish Hare
Capital City: Dublin
Currency: Euro
Language: Irish/English
National Holiday(s): March 17
Famous Landmarks:

St. Patrick's Cathedral
Trinity College
Dublin Castle
Ha'penny Bridge
Kilmainham Gaol
Blarney Castle & Stone
Cliffs of Moher
Rock of Cashel
Giant's Causeway
Newgrange Tomb

Ireland

Ireland Flag Coloring

Color the flag of Ireland the correct colors – use markers, crayons or paint.

The flag colors of Ireland include a left strip of green, a middle strip of white and a right strip of orange. Green stands for the Catholic community, orange stands for the Protestant community, and the white stands for peace.

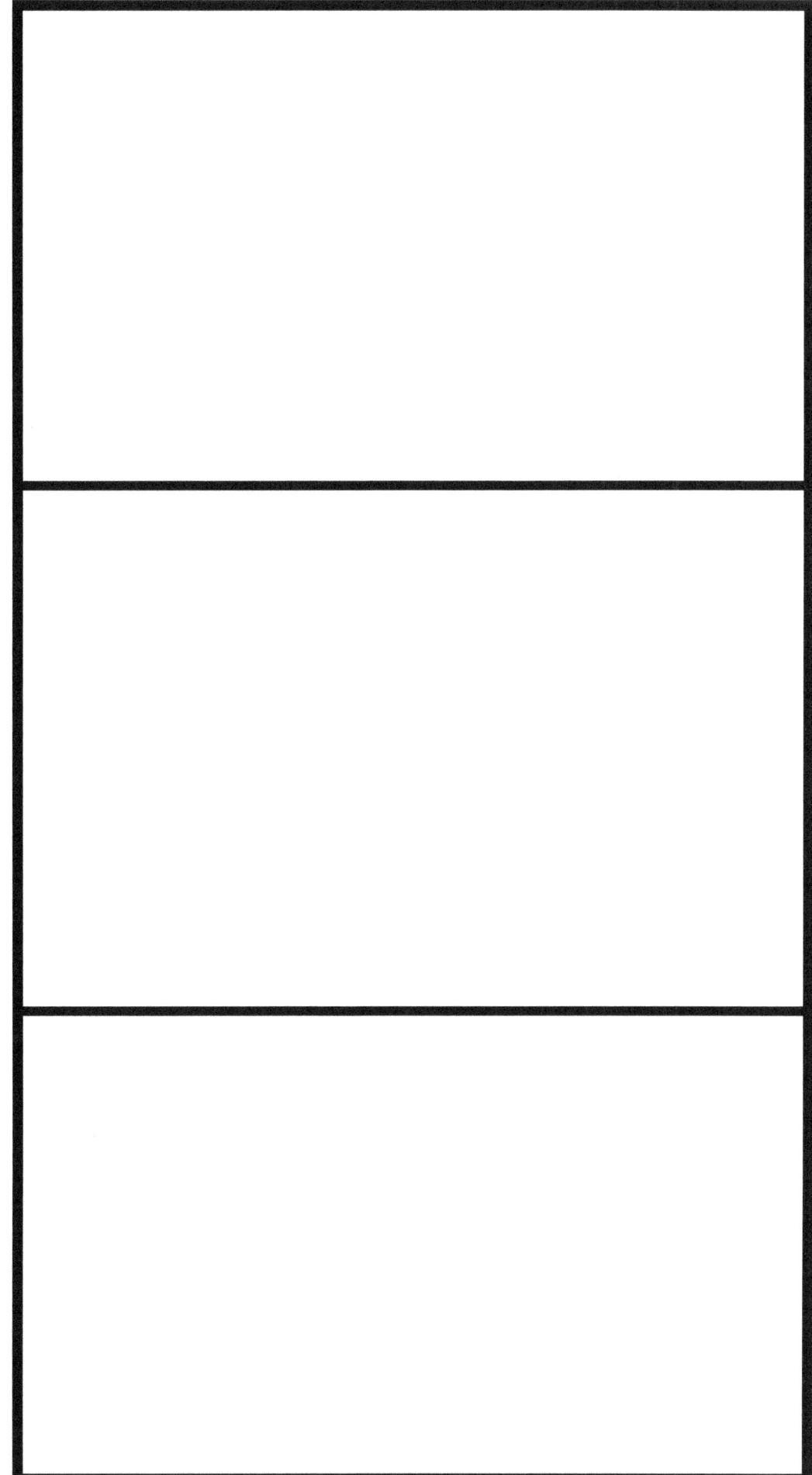

Ireland Landmarks (3-Part Cards)

Rock of Cashel

Newgrange Tomb

Blarney Stone/Castle

St. Patrick's Cathedral

Ireland Landmarks (3-Part Cards)

Rock of Cashel

Newgrange Tomb

Blarney Stone/Castle

St. Patrick's Cathedral

Ireland Landmarks (3-Part Cards)

Trinity College

Dublin Castle

Ha'Penny Bridge

Cliffs of Moher

Ireland Landmarks (3-Part Cards)

Trinity College

Dublin Castle

Ha'Penny Bridge

Cliffs of Moher

Ireland Landmarks (3-Part Cards)

Giant's Causeway **Giant's Causeway**

Kilmainham Gaol **Kilmainham Gaol**

Ireland Landmarks

Cut out circles using a 1" circle punch or scissors. Place circles on map where the landmarks are located. Refer to the control version for help if needed.

Ireland Cities

Cut out the labels and attach them to the diagram

Londonderry	Belfast	Dublin	Galway
Waterford	Cork	Limerick	Killarney
Sligo			
Westport			

Instructions

Paste included map illustration onto foamboard, cardboard or corkboard. Glue straight or T-pin to back of labels or photo circles and pin into map at appropriate location of landmark or city.

Ireland

Please note that the locations may not be exact as markers are positioned to be seen when multiple locations are in similar area.

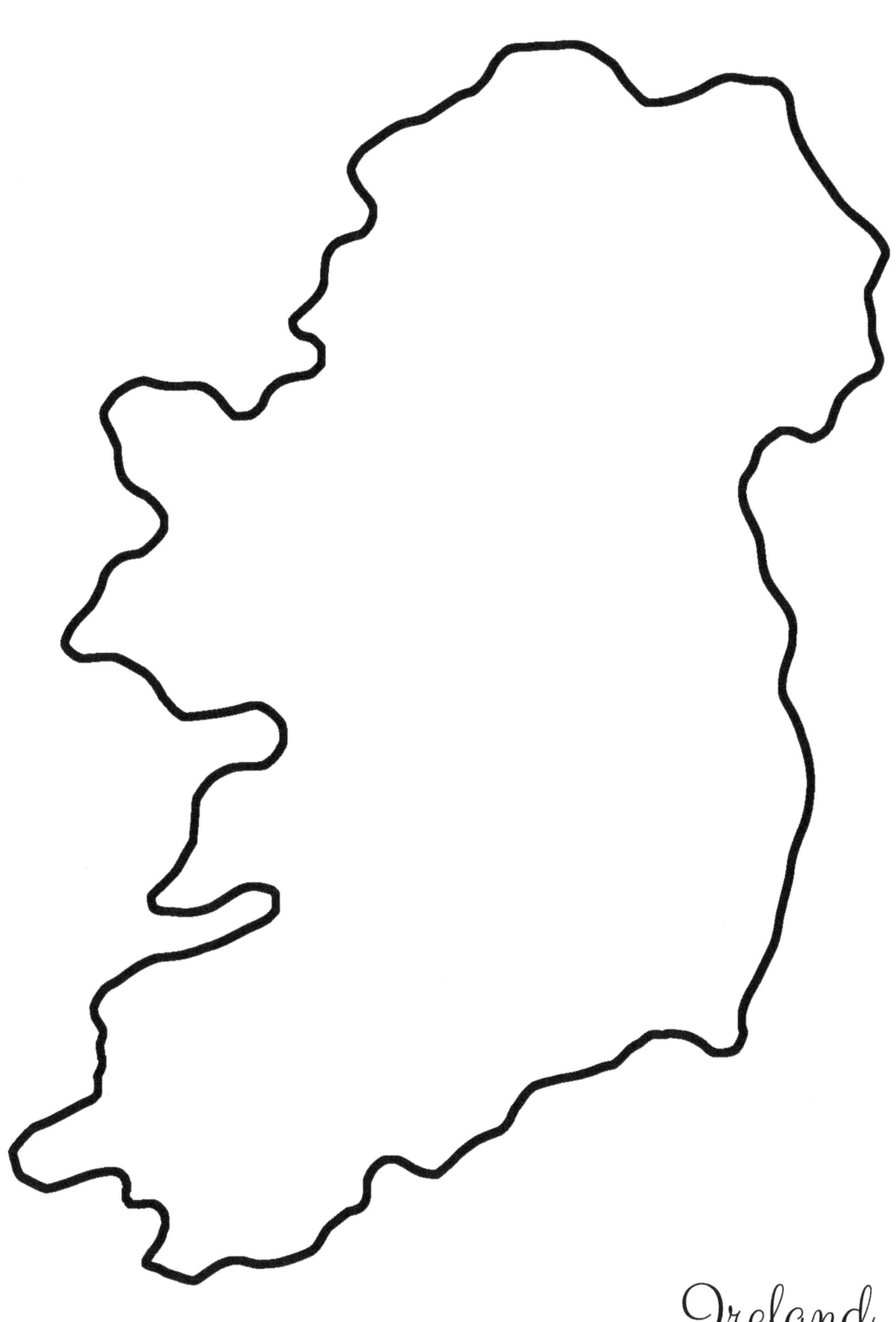

Europe Continent: Ireland

Cut out Europe continent. Glue over corkboard or cardboard. Cut out flag and glue onto toothpick or straight pin. Mark country with flag.

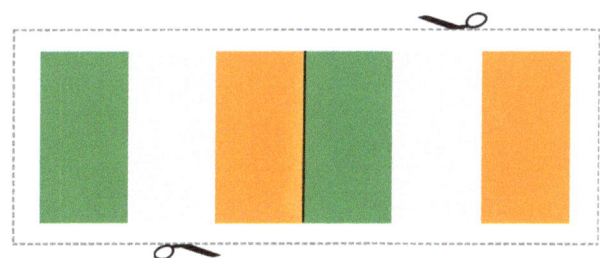

Ireland Fun Facts

Ireland was Titanic's last port of call. This historic ship was built in Belfast.

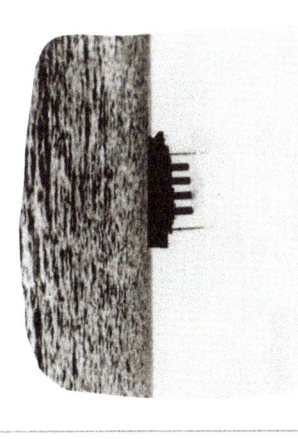

Green wasn't always associated with Ireland. St. Patrick wore light blue frequently.

The Cliffs of Moher are featured in several major movies.

Ireland is the only country with a musical instrument as a national symbol.

The first St. Patrick's Day parade was held in the USA, not Ireland.

St. Patrick wasn't actually Irish, he was born in Great Britain.

Irish Gaelic is the official language of Ireland, although very few people speak it.

The Irish flag was inspired by the French.

Ireland Fun Facts

Dublin was originally a Viking settlement.

St. Patrick didn't chase actual snakes out of Ireland, he chased pagans.

Near Dublin, there is an island with a population of wallabies, descendants from the local zoo.

Only about 10% of Irish have red hair.

There are around 30,000 castles in Ireland.

Halloween traditions as we know them began with the Celtic festival of Samhain.

Newgrange dates back to the Neolithic period, which is older than Stonehenge or the Giza Pyramids.

Ireland's nickname is the *Emerald Isle*, due to it's luscious rolling green hills.

ST. PATRICK'S CATHEDRAL MODEL

Instructions

Located in the heart of Dublin, Ireland, Saint Patrick's Cathedral was founded in 1191 as a Roman Catholic cathedral. Today it is currently the national cathedral of the Church of Ireland.

Cut out included cathedral templates. Locate the tower side 1 & 2 pieces. Fold along indicated lines and secure together with craft glue. It may be helpful to use clothespins to hold pieces in place while drying. Locate the Spire. Fold along indicated lines to create a pointed cone-shaped structure. Secure sides of Spire with craft glue along indicated tab. Secure Tower floor inside center of Tower just below the ceiling. Secure Spire onto the Tower floor so it extends upwards from the Tower center. Locate the Nave sides (north & south) and the Nave roof. Secure the sides to the roof as indicated and allow to dry completely. Use eight connector pieces (two on each side of the ends) to create tabs to adhere the Nave fronts (east and west), as indicated.

Materials
- St. Patrick's Cathedral Templates
- Scissors
- Craft Glue
- Clothespins (optional)

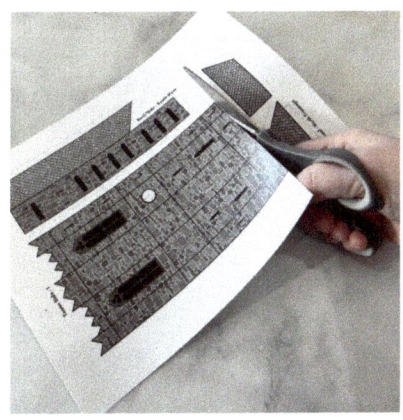

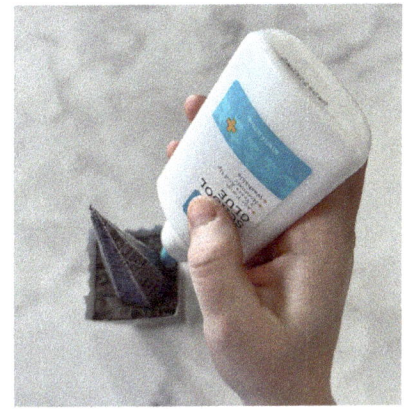

Locate the Transept front (north and south) pieces as well as the four sides and roof pieces. Assemble the north and south sides by securing the sides along the inner sides of Transept front, flush with the bottom. The windows on the side walls should be close to front. Fold the roof pieces in half and securing them to the fronts and sides with the included tabs. Secure to sides of Nave, lining up the left side of each Transept along dotted lines on Nave side. Repeat with other Transept and allow to dry completely.

Locate Nave sides walls and roof pieces (north and south). Fold roof pieces along center line and adhere to side pieces, allowing Towers to extend upwards, as indicated. Repeat with opposite side. Adhere to the east Nave front along roof with tabs and secure to sides of central Nave roof as well as the Transepts with tabs. Adjust to fit so rooflines appear straight. Locate roof side, north Nave. Adhere end to wall side of transept with tabs. Secure side roof to Nave roof and secure to sides

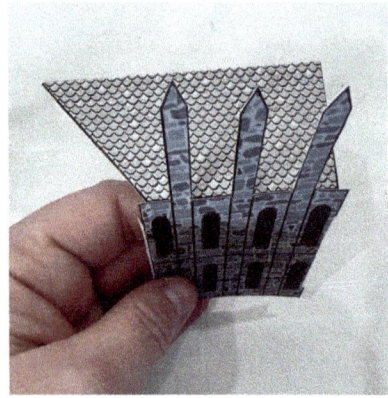

of Transept and Nave along wall with tabs.

Repeat process on south side, so both sides of the west end of the Nave are lined with the shorted sides. Allow to dry completely.

Secure Tower to left side of west front and right side of north outer wall. Locate north Nave entrance and secure between windows, as indicated. Locate south Nave entrance and secure to south Nave entrance roof. Secure to south shorter wall next to west front. Allow to dry completely.

Fold roof/side south and north Transept pieces and secure them to sides of Transept fronts and to the east Nave front on either side, using tabs.

Locate the Lady Chapel walls/front (East), roof and interior wall pieces. Fold along indicated lines and attach the interior wall to the sides of the Lady Chapel. Secure the roof to the structure using indicated tabs as well as the center seam along back of roof. Locate Lady Chapel side walls/front (North and South) and fold along indicated lines. Fold roofs along indicated lines and secure to sides and front with tabs. Attatch both Lady Chapel sides to either side of main Lady Chapel, using tabs. Allow to dry and display.

Nave Side - North

Nave Side - South

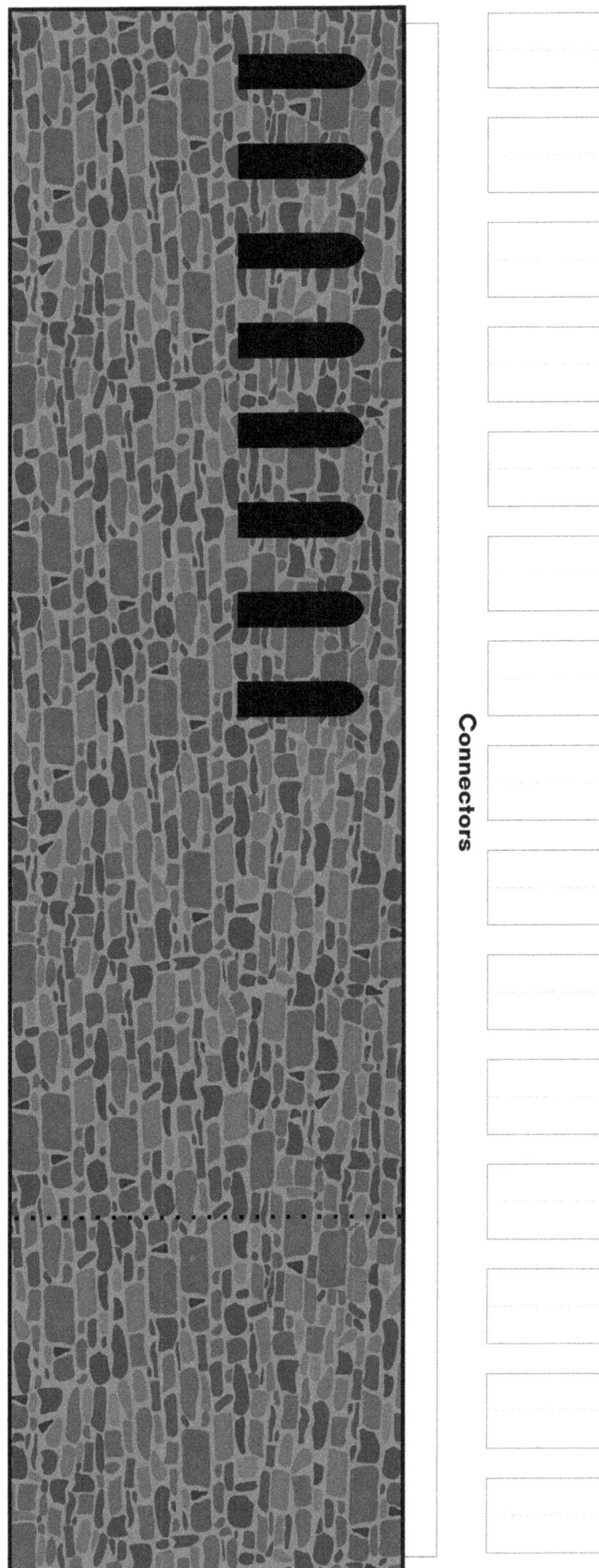

Connectors

Nave Roof

Roof/Side - South Transept

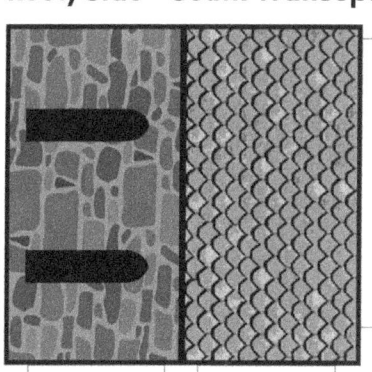

Tower Side - 1

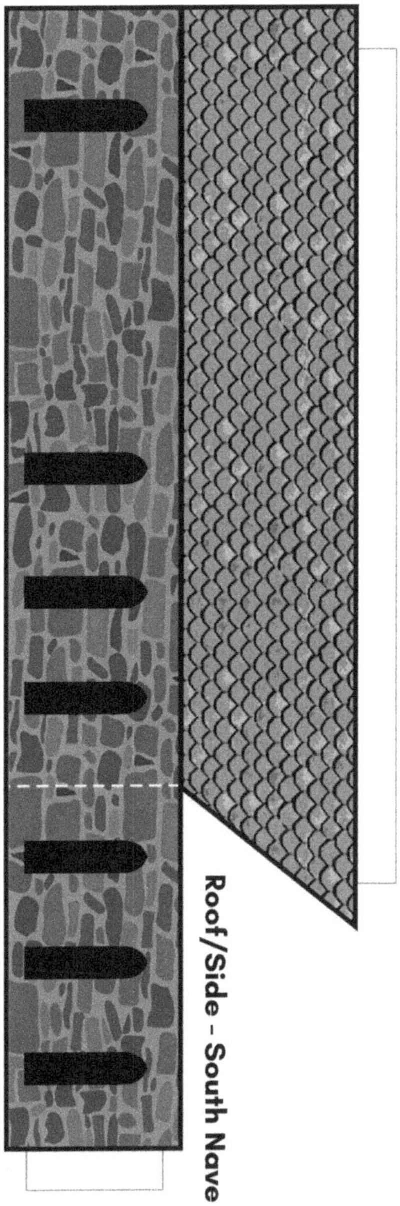

Roof/Side - South Nave

Side Roof - South Transept

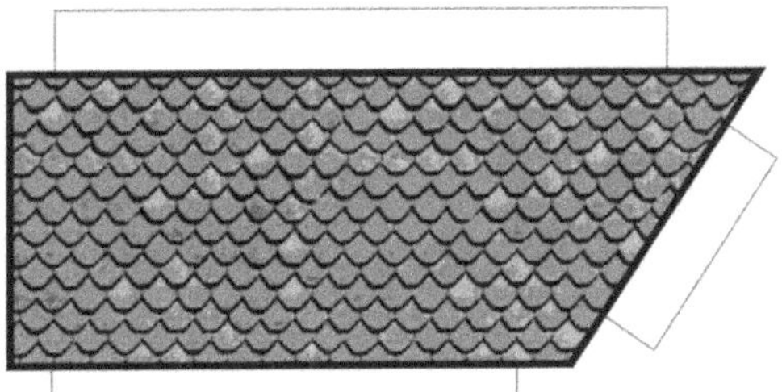

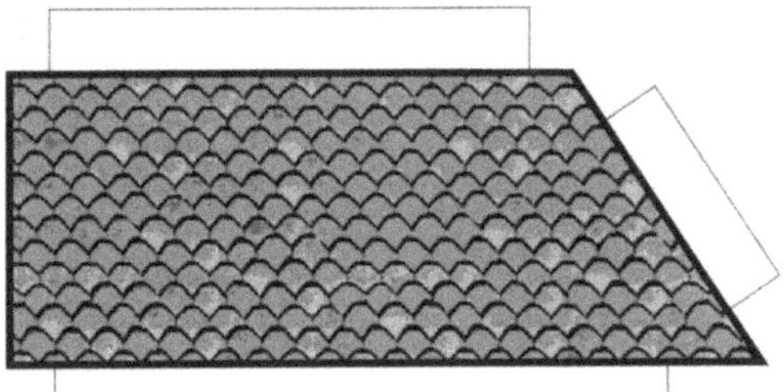

Side Roof - North Transept

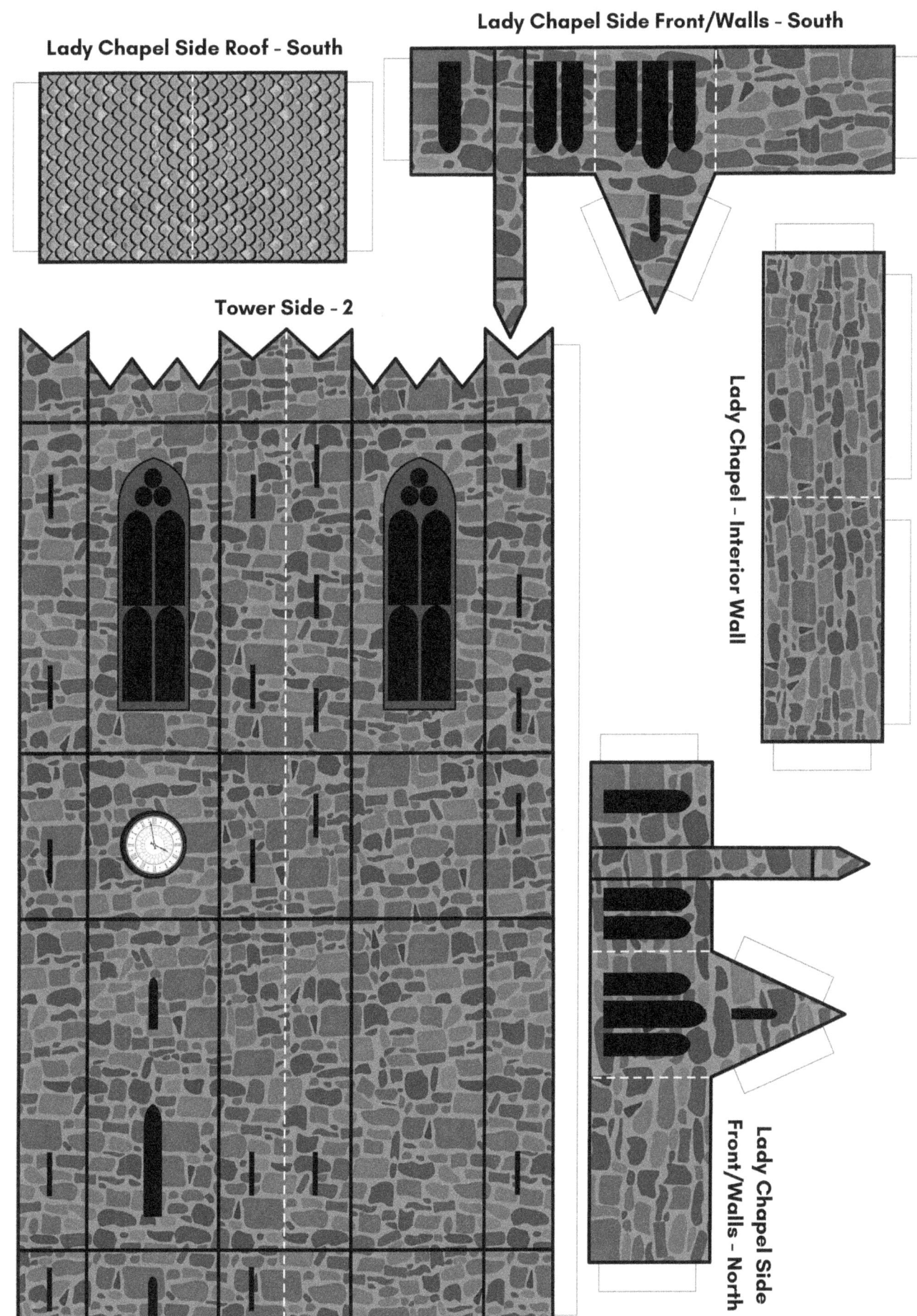

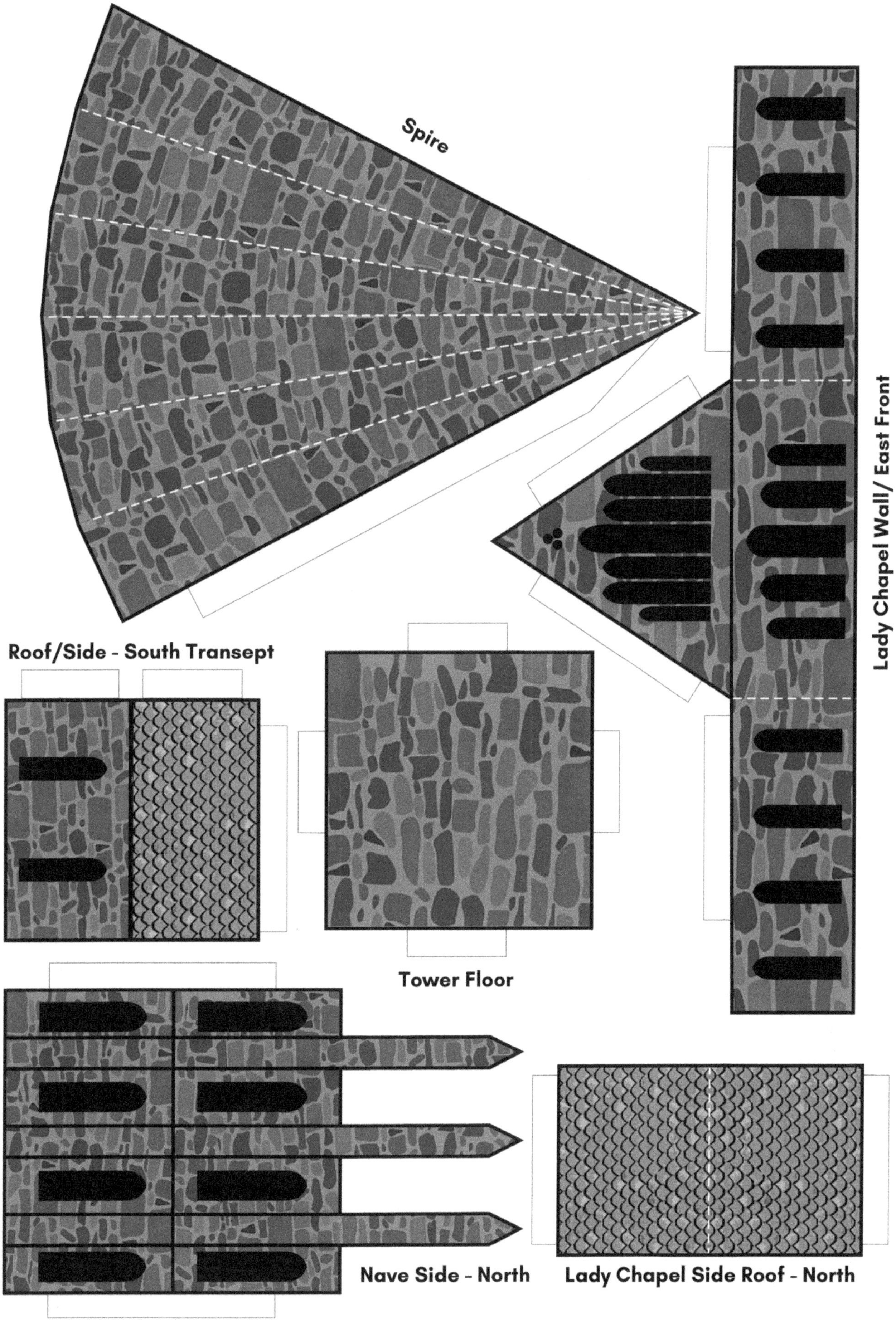

Spire

Lady Chapel Wall / East Front

Roof/Side - South Transept

Tower Floor

Nave Side - North

Lady Chapel Side Roof - North

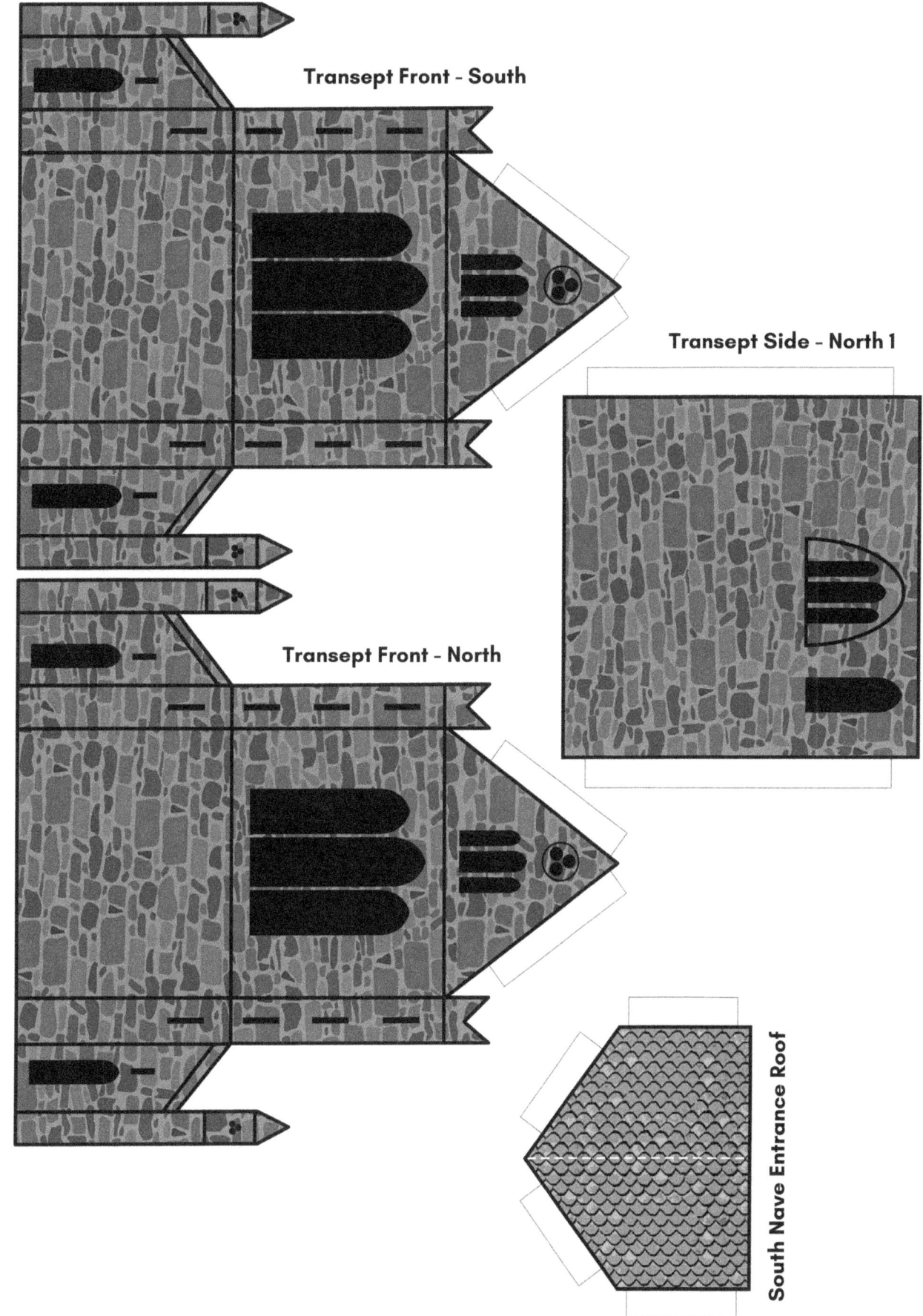

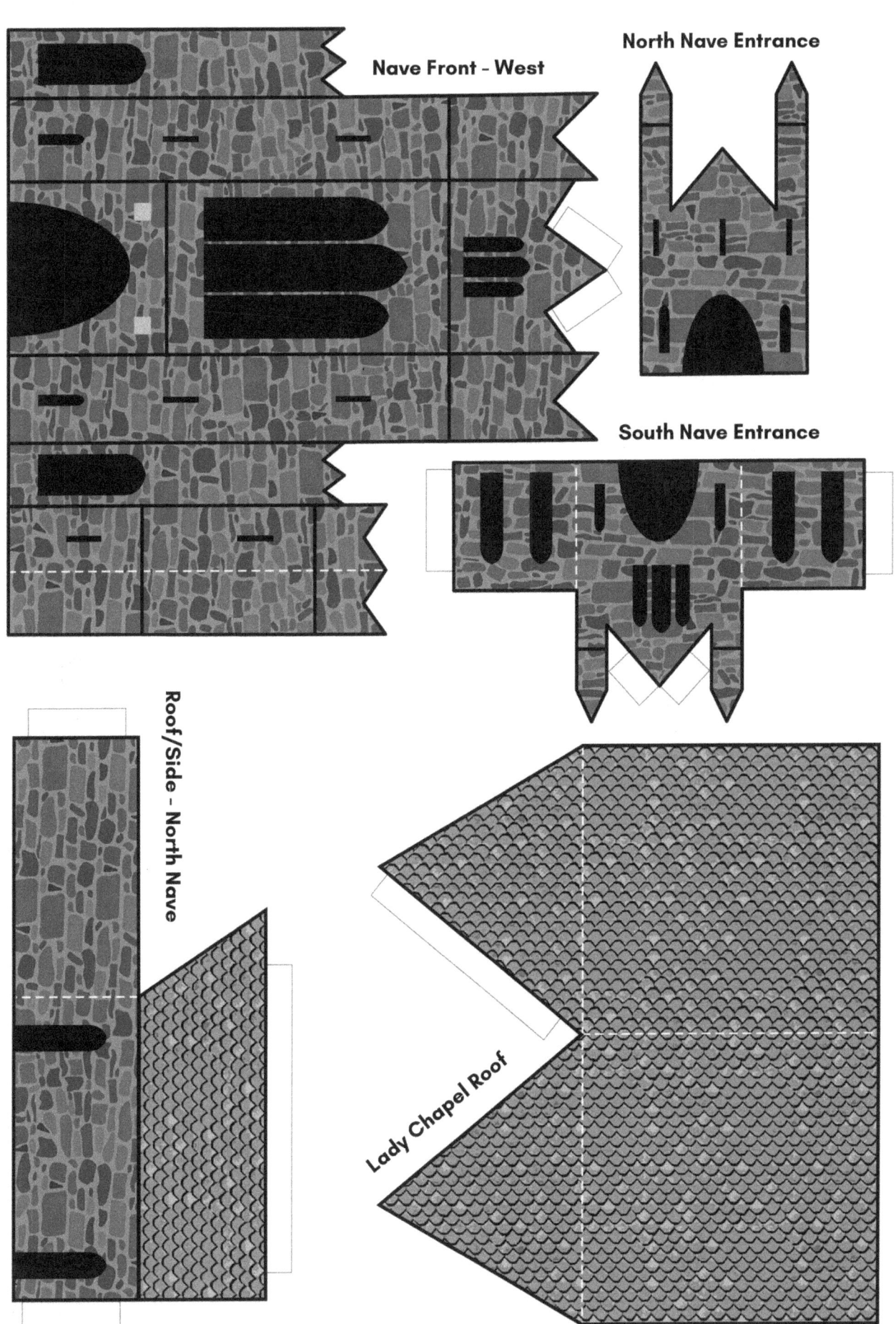

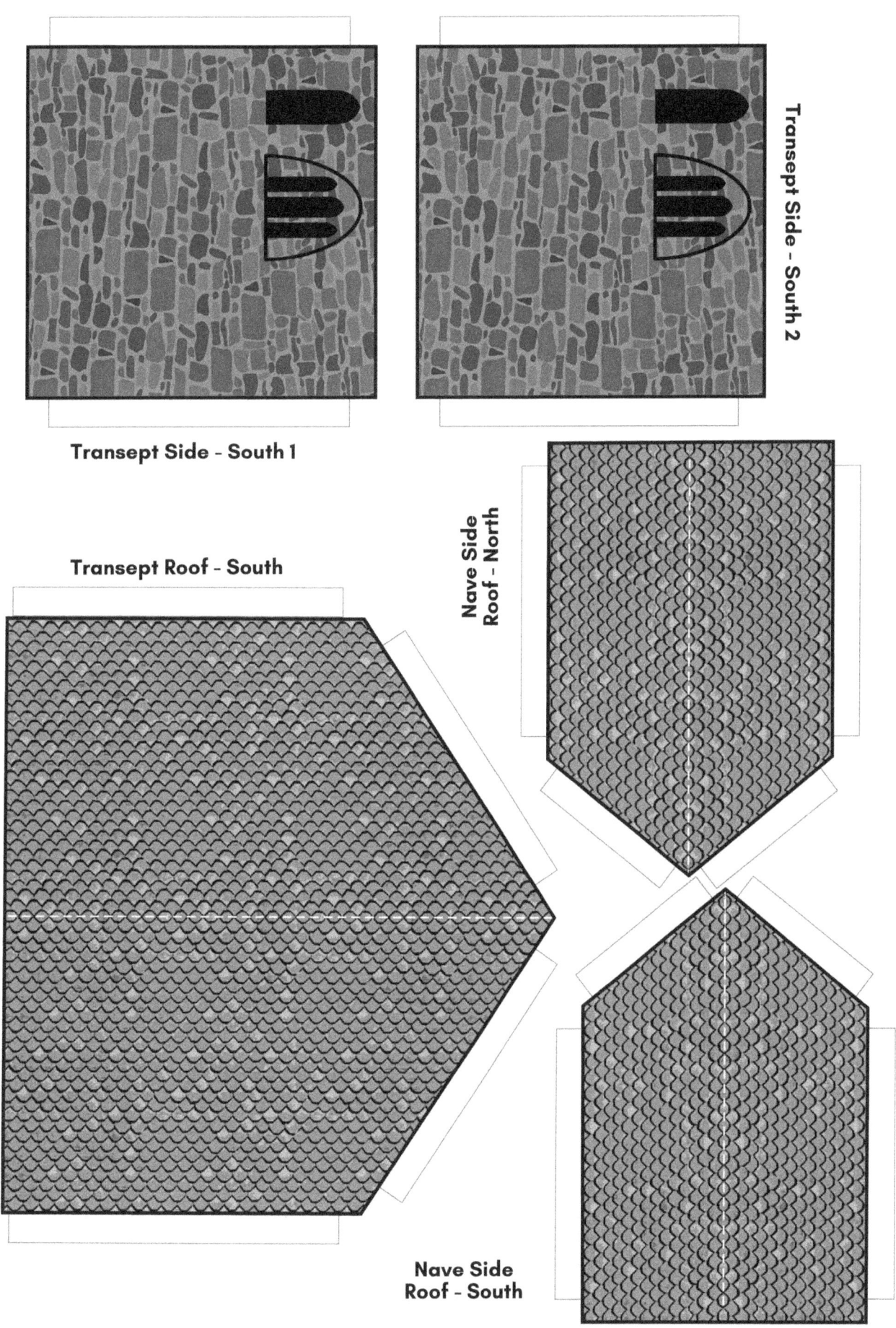

Nave Front - East

Nave Side - South

Transept Roof - North

Transept Side - North 2

ST. PATRICK & THE LOST LAMB

Maewyn was so happy to have the sheep back safe! He immediately thanked God for his blessings and promised to tell everyone about God.

Every day, Maewyn would take the sheep far up into the mountains where they could find good grass to eat.

Once upon a time, back when Saint Patrick was a boy, his name was Maewyn Succat. He would watch his family's sheep during the day.

1

From then on, Maewyn told everyone about this miracle that God had provided. He decided he would spend his life teaching people about God. He later changed his name to Patrick and his good deeds helped him become a saint.

THE END.

10

One day, a wolf found the flock of sheep and snatched one of the little lambs.

3

To Maewyn's surprise, the wolf that had stolen the sheep from the night before had came back and still had the lamb, unharmed!

8

The next day, Maewyn took the rest of the sheep back to the mountains like he did every day.

7

Quick as a flash, the wolf ran away the little lamb before Maewyn could even do anything about it.

4

Assembly Instructions

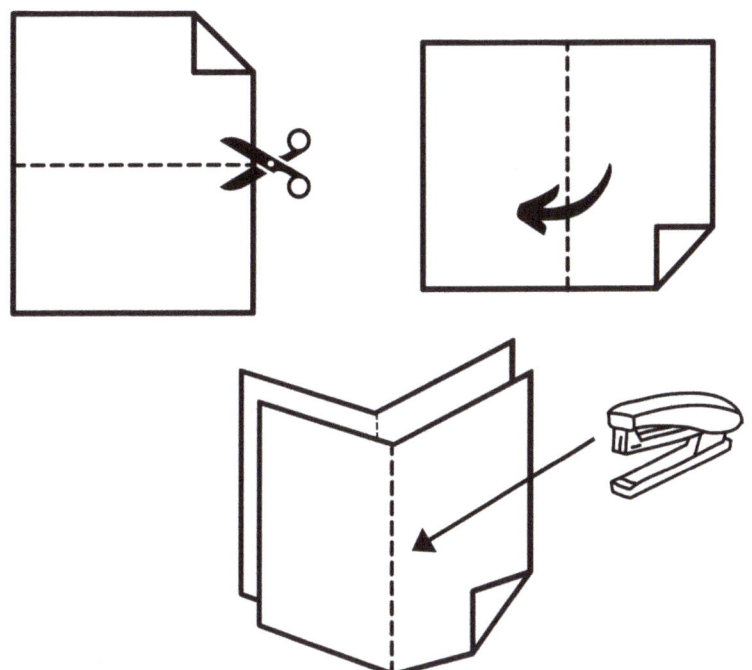

Cut paper in half on lines. Fold each page of book as indicated. Collate together so pages match up appropriately. Staple spine to hold together.

Maewyn was sad, but he had great faith in God. That night, he prayed for the little lamb and that God would keep it safe.

Maewyn slept soundly because he knew God would take care of the little lamb.

CELTIC KNOT

Materials
- 1 Yard/Meter of Cord/String (Shoelace works well too)

Instructions

The Celtic Knot is used around Ireland as both decoration and historical significance.

Provide the child a yard or meter length of cord. A shoelace will also work well for this activity. Make sure to have the ends taped to prevent unraveling. First have the child form a loop with the string, and then pass the right end through the loop from the bottom. **Note:** only the right side of the cord/string will move. Next pull the end from the top through the bottom. Finally weave it by going under the bottom cord, over the middle, under the top middle and over the top cord. Tada! Pull both ends to tighten into a beautiful knot.

Discuss: What uses would this type of knot be good for? What are some other kinds of knots you have seen? How are they different?

Celtic Symbol Tracing

Triskele - The arms spiraling out reflects a balance between inner consciousness and outer self.

Knotted Circles - Intertwined infinity symbols represent people coming together as one.

Knotwork Crosses - Celtic knotwork often interweaves to form a cross, which signifies a crossroads or meeting place.

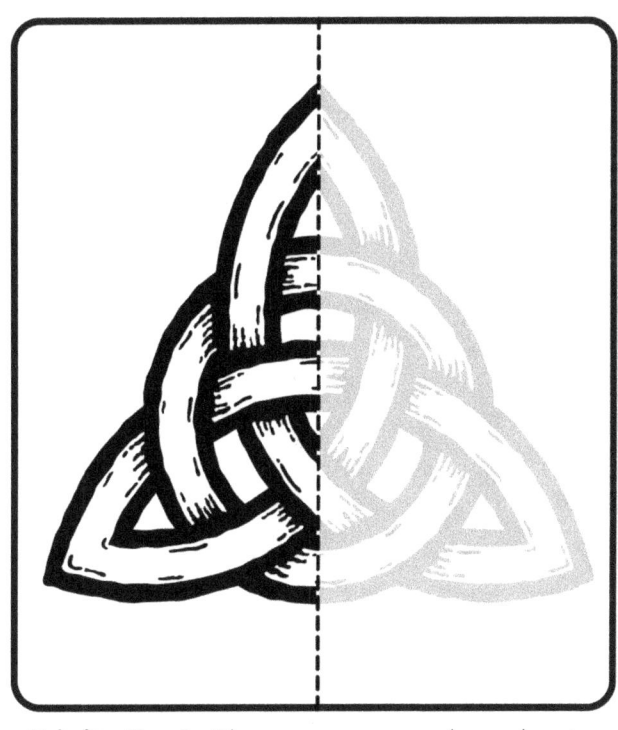

Trinity Knot - Three was a sacred number to the Celts and represents the triple aspect of Celtic gods.

Celtic Symbol Tracing

Knotwork Crosses - Celtic knotwork often interweaves to form a cross, which signifies a crossroads or meeting place.

Knotted Interlace - Interwoven knots represent how everything on Earth and in the cosmos is connected through nature.

Celtic Cross - Combines a ring around the traditional Christian cross, and represents knowledge, strength and compassion to manage life's ups and downs.

Sailor's Knot - Interwoven knots represents friendship, affection, love, and harmony. Although simple, it is also one of the strongest.

CELTIC HARP

Instructions

The Celtic harp is a triangular frame harp traditional to Ireland and Scotland. It is known as *cláirseach* in Irish, and was a wire-strung instrument requiring great skill and long practice to play. It was traditionally associated with the Gaelic ruling class.

Cut out included harp template. Use included pattern to cut out three outlines from cardboard. Secure the front and back pieces to the cardboard with glue and trim as needed. Punch holes at indicated areas along top and bottom of harp. Line up with center cardboard piece and punch holes through center piece as well. Secure all pieces together with glue and allow to dry completely. It may be helpful to use clothespins to hold pieces in place while drying and to prevent warping during drying process. Thread string through holes at top and bottom. Tie securely at back and repeat until harp is all strung. While this harp doesn't actually make music, it can be used as a prop when discussing the Irish national symbol or as a sensory activity.

Materials
- Harp Template
- Cardboard
- Craft Glue/Glue Stick
- Hole Punch
- Scissors
- String

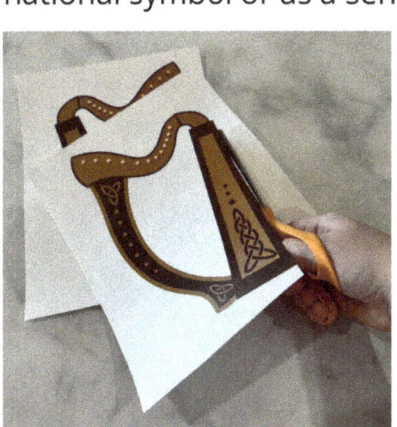

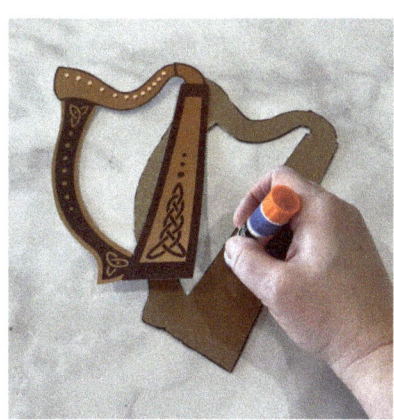

Celtic Harp

Celtic Harp

Gaelic Alphabet Cards

Gaelic Alphabet Cards

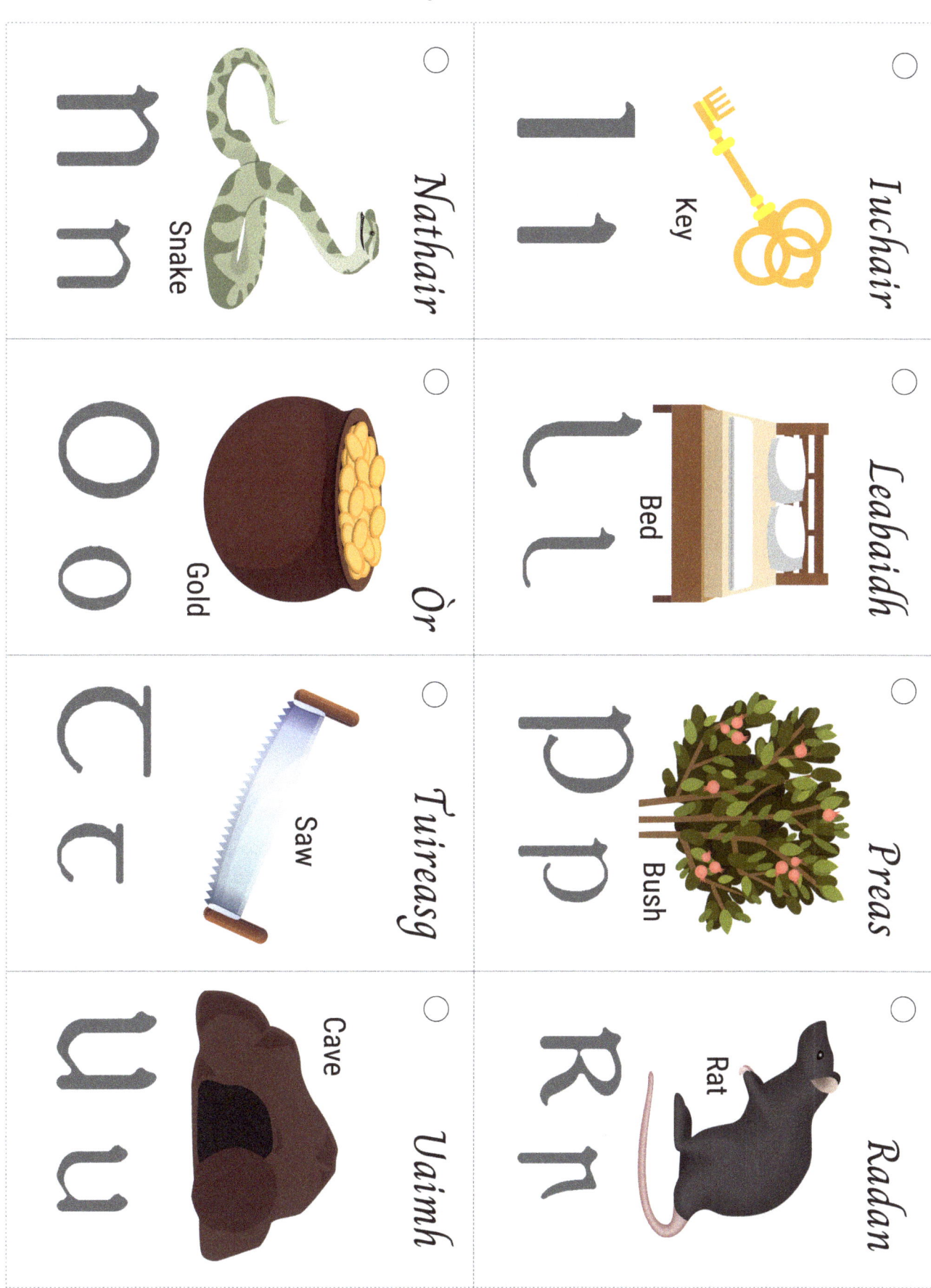

Gaelic Alphabet Cards

Potato Stamp Templates

POTATO STAMPING

Instructions

Potatoes have long since been a major part of the Irish diet. They are also excellent foundations for making fun stampers. Russet or Yams are larger and provide more surface area for the stamps, but smaller potatoes can be used for smaller designs. Use a cookie cutter or included templates to create

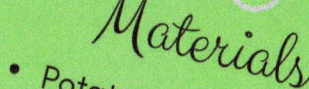

Materials
- Potatoes
- Cookie Cutters
- Outlines
- Green Paint
- Craft Paper

a design. Insert the cookie cutter or cut around the pattern with a pairing knife. Trim off the surrounding potato so that the stamper design becomes visible. Provide a smear of paint to stamp into with a flat small storage or casserole dish. Make several stampers and use different paint colors to create a pattern!

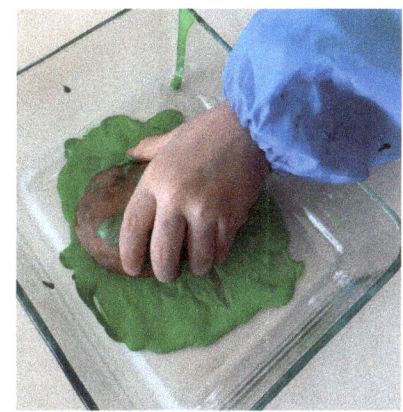

GROW A POTATO

Instructions

The Great Famine was a period of starvation in Ireland between 1845-1849. This time has also been referred to as the Irish Potato Famine as the cause was a potato blight, which infected potato crops. Growing a potato is a beautiful way to learn about the life cycle of the potato as it grows roots, leaves and ultimately becomes a plant.

Materials
- Potato
- Toothpicks
- Large Mouth Jar
- Water
- Window

First, insert tooth picks into the sides of a potato in three areas. This will keep the potato suspended above the water. You can use any kind of potato. Next, put it in a glass jar (to view the root formation) filled with water. Place the potato in the window and watch the leaves/roots form. You should see progress after only a few days. After a few weeks, leaves will emerge from the top of the jar, and you will need to plant your potato. Who knew potatoes turned into such beautiful plants?!

Varieties of Potatoes

Varieties of Potatoes

- Fingerling
- White
- Sweet
- Red

SODA BREAD

ingredients

- 4 cups all-purpose flour
- 1/4 cup white sugar
- 1 teaspoon baking soda
- 1 tablespoon baking powder
- ½ teaspoon salt
- ½ cup butter, softened
- 1 cup buttermilk
- 1 egg
- ¼ cup butter, melted
- ¼ cup buttermilk

directions

- Preheat oven to 375' F (190' C).
- Lightly grease a large baking sheet.
- In a large bowl, mix together flour, sugar, baking soda, baking powder, salt and margarine. Stir in 1 cup of buttermilk and egg.
- Continue kneading dough onto lightly floured surface for a few minutes. Form into round shape and place on prepared baking sheet.
- In a small bowl, combine melted butter with 1/4 cup buttermilk; brush loaf with this mixture. Cut a "X" into the top of the loaf with a sharp knife.
- Bake in preheated oven until a toothpick inserted into the center of the loaf comes out clean (about 45-50 minutes).

Adult Supervision Required

Soda Bread
INGREDIENTS

FLOUR — SUGAR — BAKING SODA

  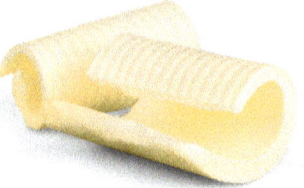

BAKING POWDER — SALT — BUTTER, SOFTENED

BUTTERMILK — EGG

COLORED CANDY RAINBOW EXPERIMENT

Materials
- Colored Candy
- Plate
- Water

Instructions

Leprechauns are associated strongly with Irish myth and legend. It is said they hide their gold at the end of rainbows.

This fun science experiment creates a rainbow of colors and what colors they make when blended together.

Line colored candy around the edge of a medium to large plate. The more colors the better. Slowly pour warm water into the middle of the plate until it touches all the candy. Wait as the coloring from the candy fills the plate.

Discuss: What colors are made by adjacent colors combining? Do they fade over time? Talk about what you see.

RAINBOW POPSICLES

Instructions

Popsicles are a beloved summer treat and often enjoyed year round. This fun (and healthy) activity makes natural rainbow colored popsicles and allows children to learn valuable practical life skills.

To begin, choose fruits that are naturally the desired colors. Red can be made from strawberries, raspberries, watermelon, etc. Oranges and mango are orange. Pineapple makes yellow. Blend with banana to help tone down the acidity if desired. Kiwi is a good green, or mix a couple leaves of spinach for extra nutrients to give a bolder green color. Blueberries make a good "blue" which is slightly purple. And blackberries, grapes, etc., make a good purple. Be creative if desired with different colors.

Using a popsicle mold, fill the bottom with just a tiny amount of the first color. Allow to freeze for about an hour before adding the second. If using pureed fruit (instead of juice), adding all the colors at the same time can be done, but freezing in between creates a stark contrast. After completely frozen, enjoy! What a fun way to learn about the rainbow!

Materials
- Assorted Fruit Juices
- Popsicle Mold
- Freezer

IRISH STEP-DANCING

Materials
- Video of an Irish Step Dance

Instructions

The Irish stepdance is a dance style that is traditionally associated with Irish culture. It is generally characterized by a stiff upper body and fast and precise movements of the feet. It can be performed solo or in groups. The footwork usually includes the balls of the feet with toes pointed outwards, and the moves include a rigid torso, rapid and intricate footwork, and legs and feet crossed over each other, with knees close together. This activity has excellent gross motor skills development.

Suggestion: Watch a video of the Irish stepdance and attempt to recreate the moves. Ask: Is it hard to only move your lower body? Can you keep up with the fast moves?

Leprechaun Photo Prop

Cut out hat and beard. Glue or tape to a craft stick. Place in front of face and snap a selfie!

Leprechaun Photo Prop

Pot 'O Gold Counting

Leprechauns and their pots of gold are traditionally associated with Irish culture. Cut out the numbered pots, square tally cards and gold coins. Have the child match the number on the pot with the appropriate number of gold pieces, and the tally cards that go with it. Try different numbers. See if the child can match all the pots to their associated cards.

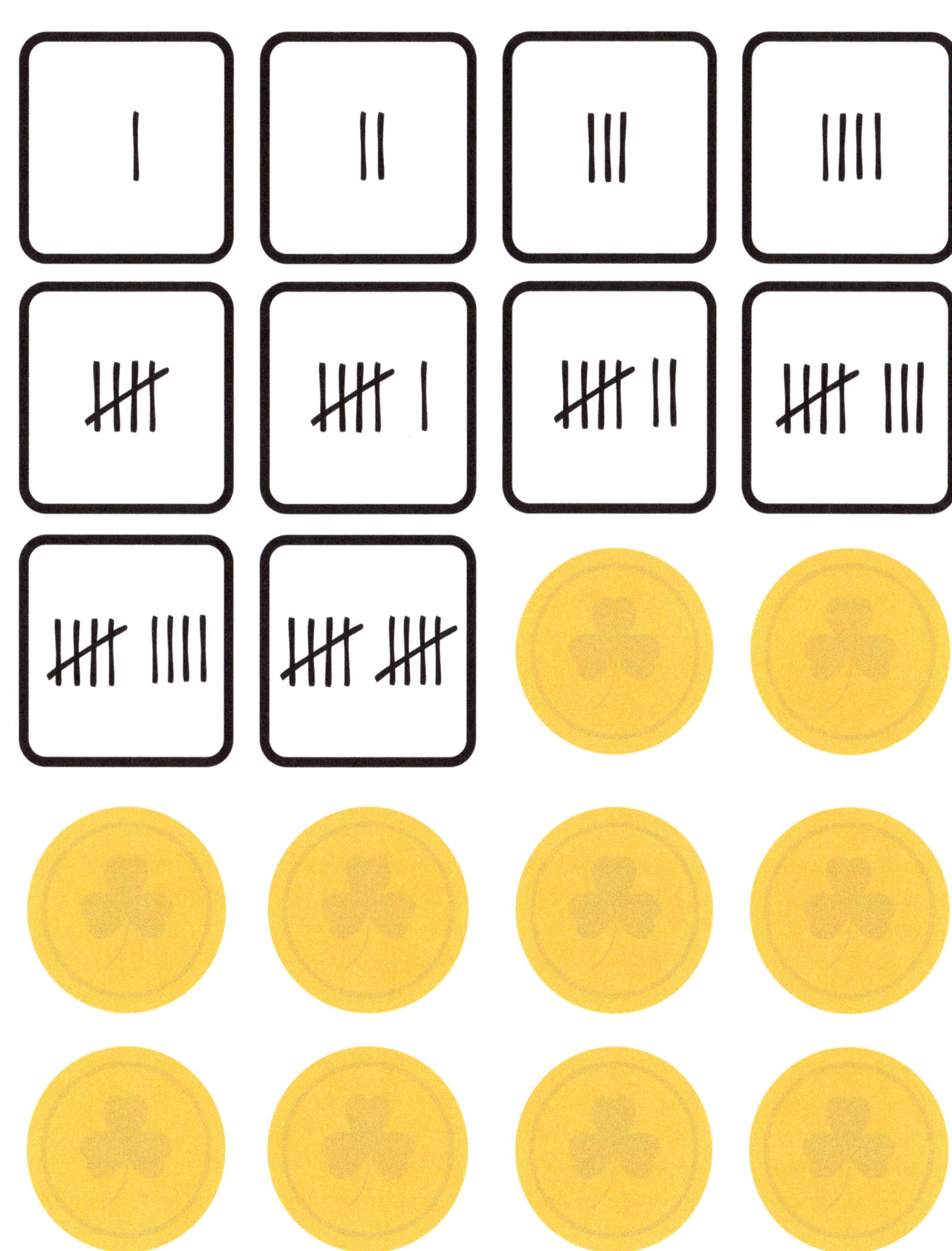

Leprechaun Maze

Help the Leprechaun find his pot of gold.

"Green" Nature Hunt

PUNNETT SQUARES

Instructions

Red hair is often associated with Ireland with approximately 10% of the Irish population having red hair (compared to only 1-2% worldwide). Red hair is a recessive trait, which means that only those who get two "redhead" versions of the gene, one from the mother and one from the father, will have red hair. The Punnett square is a square diagram used to predict the genetics. It was named after Reginald C. Punnett, who devised the approach in 1905.

Materials
- Punnett Squares Template
- Pen/Pencil
- Dominate/Recessive Trait List

Choose two genes from the included list. Identify if the gene is recessive or dominant. Use a letter to indicate the gene and fill it in on the dashed lines above and to the left of the square for the "mother" and the "father" - it doesn't matter if you choose recessive or dominate or a combination of both. Indicate recessive genes as lower-case letters and dominate genes as upper case letters. Next, assign the first letter of the Mother and the first letter of the Father to the upper left green square (the grey separates the squares). Then repeat with the first letter of the mother and the second letter of the father in the upper right square. Continue with the second letter of the mother and first letter of the father in the bottom left square and with the second letter of both parents in the bottom right square.

Next circle each pair of letters that match. What combinations do you have? Mark the percentage of each combination identified. Remember that recessive traits are not expressed if the individual also carries a dominant trait. Repeat with different combinations - do the percentages change? Consider your own family tree - can you identify the combinations you may have, based on your parents and yourself and/or siblings?

B = Brown Hair
r = Red Hair

BB = Brown Hair 0%
Br = Brown Hair 50%
rr = Red Hair 50%
rB = Brown Hair 0%

Mother: B, r
Father: r, r

	r	r
B	Br	Br
r	rr	rr

Punnett Squares

Punnett Squares

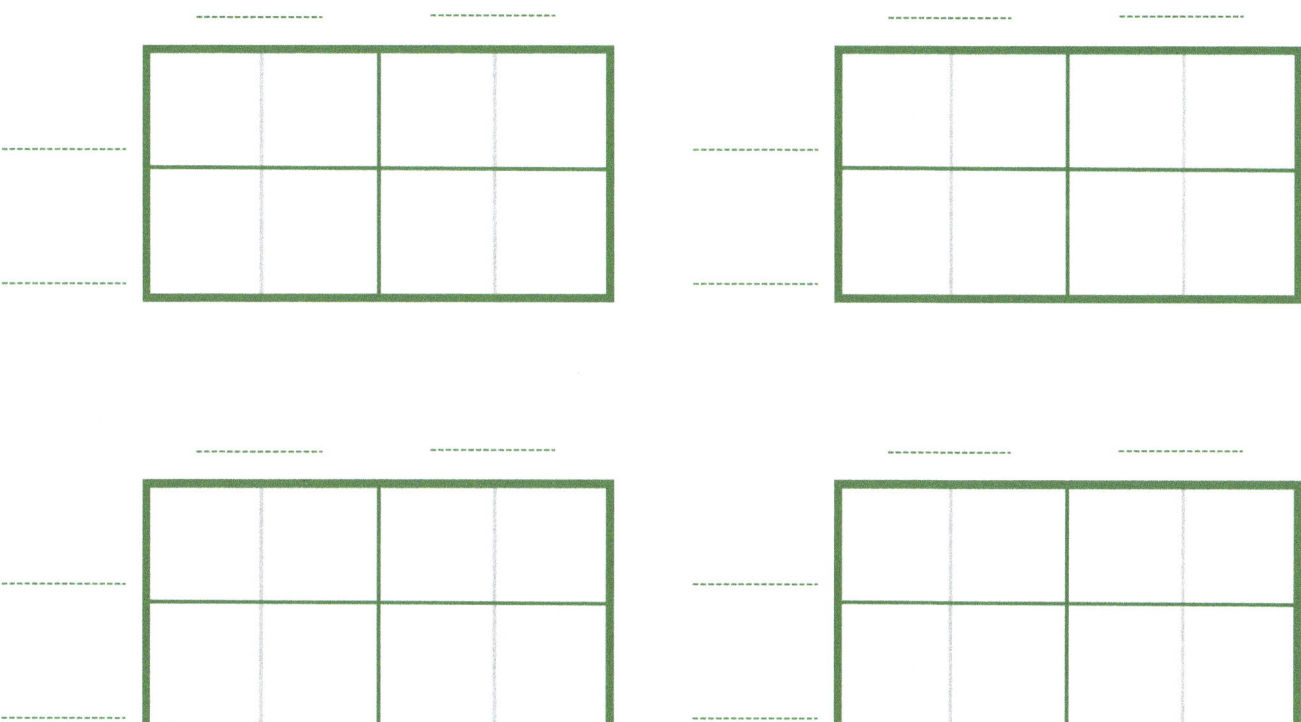

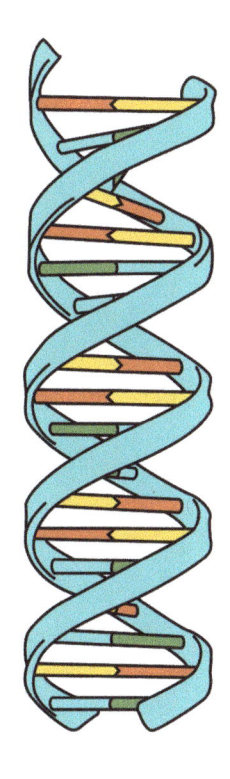

Traits	Dominant	Recessive
Baldness (in males)	Presence	Absence
Body hair	Abundant	Little
Bent pinkie	Able to bend	Not able to bend
Blood pressure rate	High	Low
Chin Cleft	Absence	Presence
Crossing of thumbs	Left thumb over right thumb	Right thumb over left thumb
Dimples	Presence	Absence
Earlobes	Definite free earlobes	Attached earlobes
Eyelash length	Long eyelash	Short eyelash
Eye Color	Brown	Blue
Freckles	Presence	Absence
Hairline	Widow's peak	Straight
Hair color	White hair streak	Uniform hair color
Hair color	Darker	Lighter
Hair Type	Curly	Straight
Handedness	Right handedness	Left handedness
Hitchhiker's thumbs	Absence	Presence
Lips width	Broad lips	Thin lips
Mid-digital hair	Presence	Absence
Mongolian eye fold	Presence	Absence
Nose shape	Roman nose (bump)	Straight
Nose width	Broad nose	Narrow nose
Number of fingers	Six fingers	Five fingers
Rh factor in blood	Rh factor positive (+)	Rh factor negative (-)
Toe length	Second toe longer than first toe	First toe longer than second toe
Tone hearing	Tone deafness	Normal hearing
Tongue rolling (side edges up)	Ability to roll tongue	Inability to roll tongue
Vision	Astigmatism	Normal vision
Webbed fingers	Presence	Absence

CLADDAGH CARD

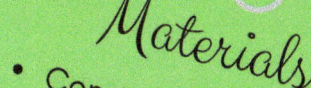

Materials
- Construction Paper
- Claddagh Templates Outlines
- Scissors
- Glue Stick

Instructions

The Claddagh symbol has centuries of Irish history, but today it symbolizes friendship, loyalty and love. Traditionally used in rings, this symbol has become synonymous with Irish culture.

Trace around the child's hand onto a folded sheet of colored paper; cut out into two hand prints. Using the accompanied illustrations, cut out a heart and a crown in contrasting colors. Use the glue stick to paste them on another sheet of construction paper with the hands holding the heart with the crown over. Write a note and send as a card or display as art.

Discuss: What are some symbols you can think of? What do they symbolize? Do some symbols mean different things in different cultures?

 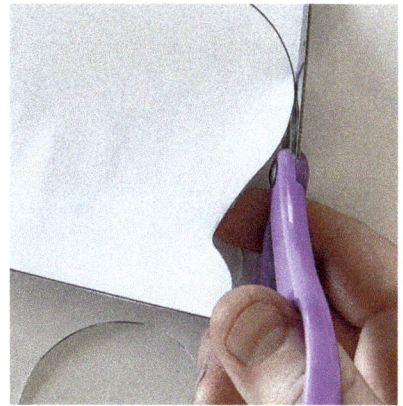 

Shamrock & Claddagh Patterns

MELTED STRAW SHAMROCK

Instructions

Shamrocks are iconic to Irish culture and history. The word shamrock derives from the Irish seamróg, meaning "young clover".

Provide child with a handful of plastic straws. To promote good habits, use straws that have been upcycled; make sure they are clean and completely dry first though. Use more than one color for a mosaic pattern. Cut each straw into small pieces. Place the straw pieces between two layers of parchment paper. Using iron on high heat, iron until pieces have melted together into plastic sheet. **Note:** This step must be completed by an adult, or under close supervision by an adult to avoid burns. Allow plastic piece to cool. Trace included shamrock outline onto the plastic and cut out. Save the left over pieces to make another one. Punch a hole in the top and hang as a decoration.

Materials
- Green Plastic Straws
- Scissors
- Parchment Paper
- Iron
- Hole Punch
- String

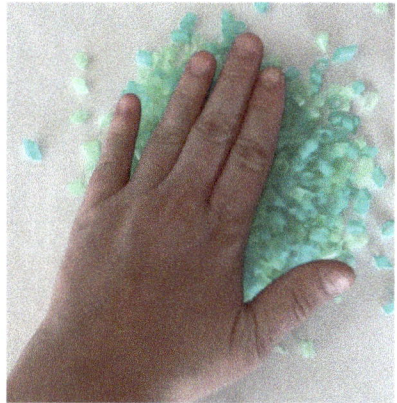
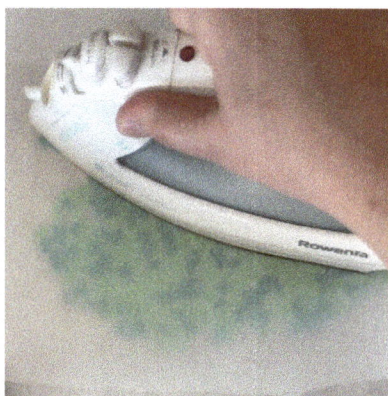

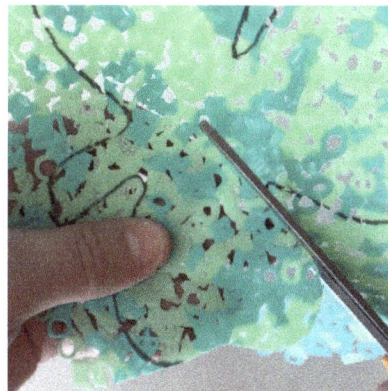

Shamrock Blessings

I'M LUCKY BECAUSE....

Name:

Cut out shamrocks and write what the child is thankful for, and hang to remind child of their blessings.

I'M LUCKY BECAUSE....

Name:

Irish Blessing Cards

May the road rise up to meet you.
May the wind be always at your back.
May the sun shine warm upon your face,
the rains fall soft upon your fields.
And, until we meet again,
may God hold you in the palm of His hand.

May peace and plenty bless your world
with a joy that long endures.
And may all life's passing seasons
bring the best to you and yours.

Irish Blessing Cards

May the raindrops fall lightly on your brow.
May the soft winds freshen your spirit.
May the sunshine brighten your heart
May the burdens of the day rest
  lightly upon you.
And may God enfold you in
  the mantle of His love.

May the friendships you make,
Be those which endure,
And all of your grey clouds
Be small ones for sure.
And trusting in Him
To Whom we all pray,
May a song fill your heart,
Every step of the way.

Life Cycle Spinner

Life Cycle of the *Shamrock*

leaflet

seeding head

flower head

stolon

petiole

Life Cycle Spinner

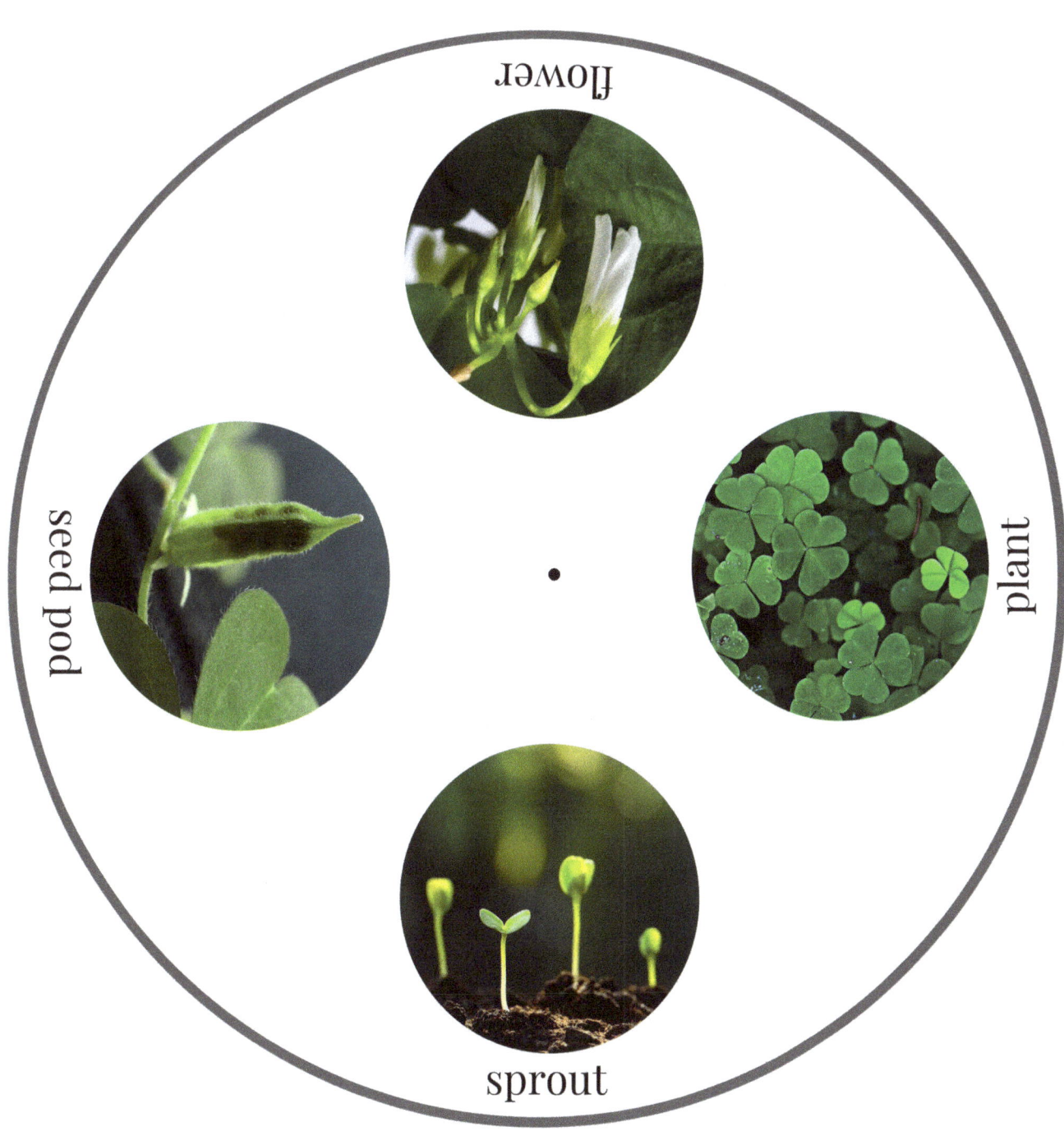

Parts of a Shamrock

Parts of a Shamrock

Learning to Write

Shamrock

Shamrock
Shamrock
Shamrock

Shamrock   Shamrock
Shamrock   Shamrock
Shamrock   Shamrock
Shamrock   Shamrock
Shamrock   Shamrock

GAME OF RINGS

Instructions

The game of 'Rings' is a traditional Irish game, played by children and adults alike. Players use a board with scoring numbers on it and rubber rings to "attach" to the board and score. Players take turns and the one with the highest score wins the match. Using the accompanied illustration, cut out board and paste onto foam board or card board. Use two layers for durability. Using long handled push pins, make "hooks" on indicated dots below numbers. Use a small dab of craft glue under pin before pushing it in to make it secure. Glue a string hook onto the back. Hang on wall and have a tournament, using hair ties as the rubber rings!

Discuss: What are some other precision games that use rings? How are they similar to this game? How are they different?

Materials
- Ring Board Template
- Glue Stick
- Craft Glue
- Foamboard/Cardboard
- Thumb Tacks
- Flexible Hair Ties

Irish Game of Rings

Ireland Fauna (3-Part Cards)

Irish Hare

Galway Sheep

Irish Wolfhound

European Hedgehog

Ireland Fauna (3-Part Cards)

Irish Hare

Galway Sheep

Irish Wolfhound

European Hedgehog

Ireland Fauna (3-Part Cards)

River Otter

Badger

Red Fox

Pygmy Shrew

Ireland Fauna (3-Part Cards)

River Otter **Badger**

Red Fox **Pygmy Shrew**

Temperate Deciduous Forest

Climate
This climate cycles through four seasons. Leaves change color in autumn, fall off in the winter, and grow back in the spring, allowing plants to survive cold winters. Average temperature is relatively mild compared to colder biomes.

Flora
There are a many different plant species in this biome. Most have three levels of plants. Lichen, moss, ferns, wildflowers and other small plants can be found on the forest floor. Shrubs fill in the middle level and hardwood trees like maple, oak, birch, magnolia, sweet gum and beech make up the third level.

Fauna
Many animals live in the temperate deciduous forest, making it a haven for wildlife. Species include foxes, deer, coyotes, bats, hawks, bears, woodpeckers and many migratory birds living among the trees. The forest floor provides shelter for many insects, spiders and reptiles.

Water
This biome is second in rainfall to the rainforests, so the climate, averaging 30 to 60 inches of precipitation a year in the form of rain and snow. Humidity ranges 60% to 80%. Water sources include rivers and their tributaries and forest ponds.

Temperate Deciduous Forest Matching

Cut out the circles of the animals founds in the *Temperate Deciduous Forest* and match into appropriate place.

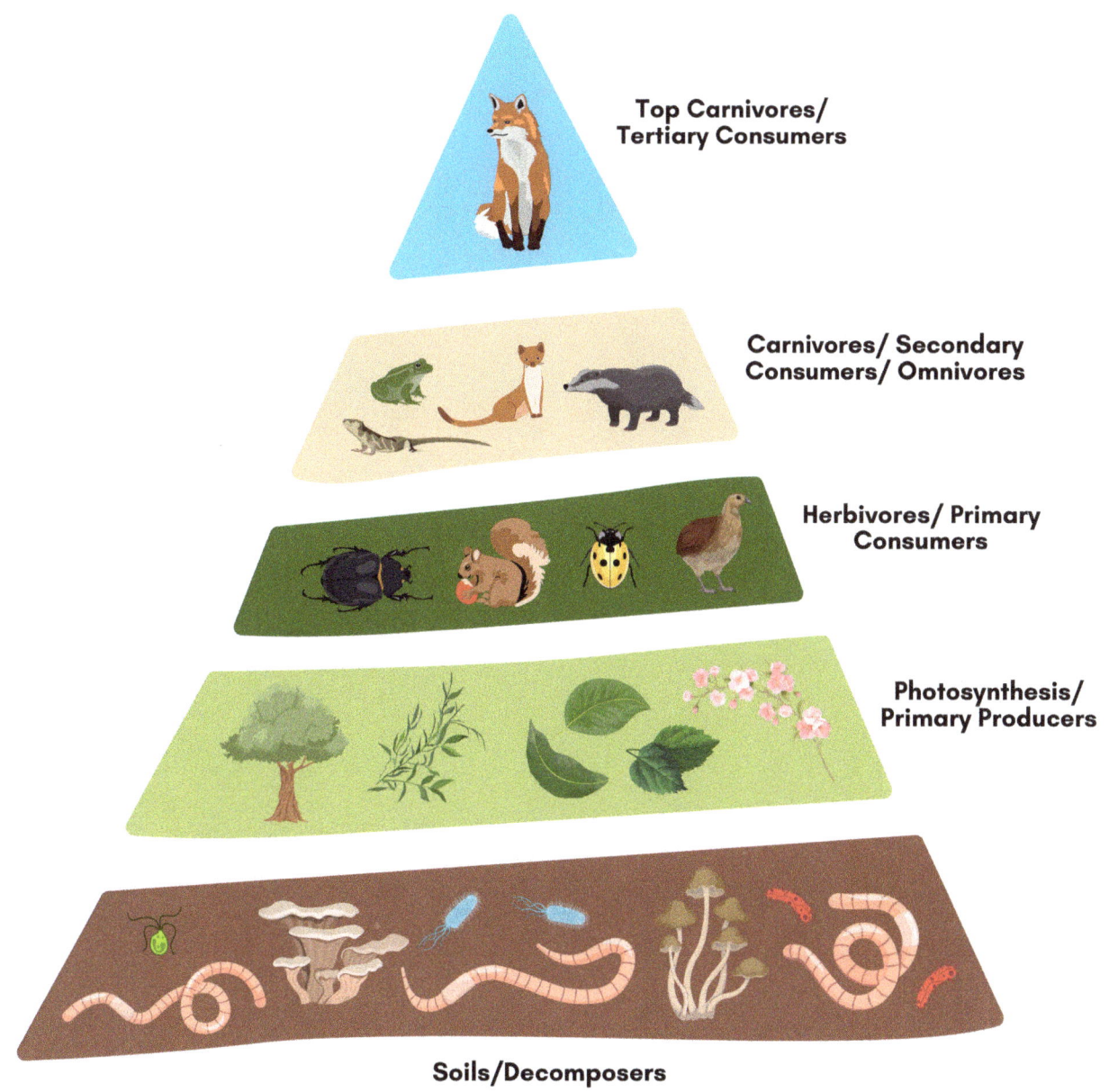

Trophic Levels
Temperate Deciduous Forest

- Top Carnivores/ Tertiary Consumers
- Carnivores/ Secondary Consumers/ Omnivores
- Herbivores/ Primary Consumers
- Photosynthesis/ Primary Producers
- Soils/Decomposers

In the *temperate deciduous forest*, there is a food web that consists of trophic (food) levels. Each trophic level has organisms that serve the same role and energy sources.

Layers of the Temperate Deciduous Forest

Ground Layer **Herb Layer**

Shrub Layer **Canopy Layer**

Ireland Currency
European currency or Euro €

The Euro € is the main unit of the European currency. The cent is a subdivision worth up to 1/100 of a Euro €.

Ireland Currency
European currency or Euro €

The Euro € is the main unit of the European currency. The cent is a subdivision worth up to 1/100 of a Euro €.

Ireland Currency
European currency or Euro €

The Euro € is the main unit of the European currency. The cent is a subdivision worth up to 1/100 of a Euro €.

Ireland Currency
European currency or Euro €

The Euro € is the main unit of the European currency. The cent is a subdivision worth up to 1/100 of a Euro €.

TITANIC MODEL

Instructions

The **RMS Titanic** was a British passenger ocean liner, operated by the White Star Line. The Titanic was built in Belfast, Ireland, but sank into the North Atlantic Ocean on April 15, 1912 after striking an iceberg during her maiden voyage from Southampton, England, to New York City, United States. Of the estimated 2,224 passengers and crew aboard, more than 1,500 died, making it the deadliest sinking of a single ship to date. Today it remains the deadliest peacetime sinking of an ocean liner or cruise ship.

Materials
- Titanic Template
- Scissors
- Craft Glue
- Clothespins (optional)
- Craft Knife
- Bamboo Sticks
- String

Cut out the included template pieces. Fold the hull pieces in half. Glue the stern and bow sides of hull and deck together along center tabs. Note: It may be helpful to use clothespins to hold the pieces in place while drying. Fold the funnels into a circular shape and glue along opposite end, as illustrated. Allow all pieces to dry completely.

Using a craft knife, cut holes as indicated at funnel insertion points along the bridge

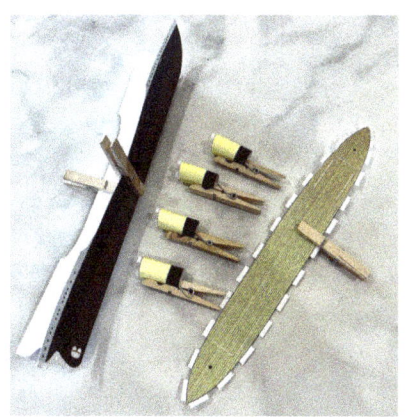
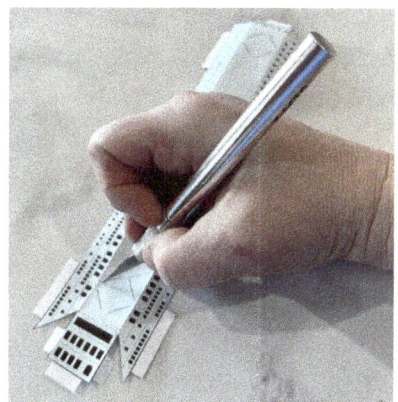
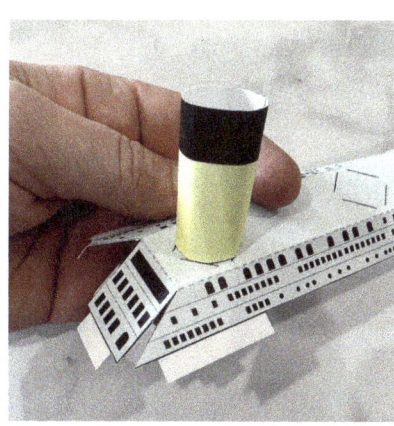

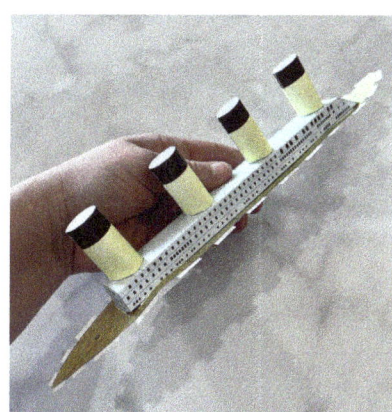

& superstructure. Note: This step should be completed by an adult or closely monitored to ensure safety. Insert tabs on bottom of funnels into the insertion points down the center. Secure tabs on opposite side, as indicated. Fold bridge/superstructure sides along indicated lines and glue together along sides to create a raised structure. Allow to dry completely. Using a craft knife, cut along indicated lines on the deck. Insert bridge/superstucture into the slits and secure tabs below the deck. Bend tabs along sides of deck downwards. Glue hull around the

perimeter of the hull, lining the top of the deck along the black portion of the ship. Work around slowly to ensure proper placement. It may be helpful to glue this portion in steps to prevent un-intended movement. Glue hull closed with tabs on bow and stern sides.

 Cut out display stands. Fold each in half and glue end pieces inside one end of each, as indicated. Glue the display card on the opposite end and allow to dry completely. Cut out propellers and glue on either side of stern side. Place inside stand. Cut two mast pole template and insert in front and back of boat. Glue string between both mast pole. Glue two smaller pieces of string from the top of each mast poles, securing them to the starboard and port side. Allow to dry and display proudly!

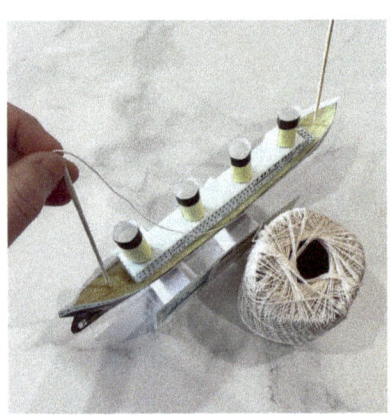

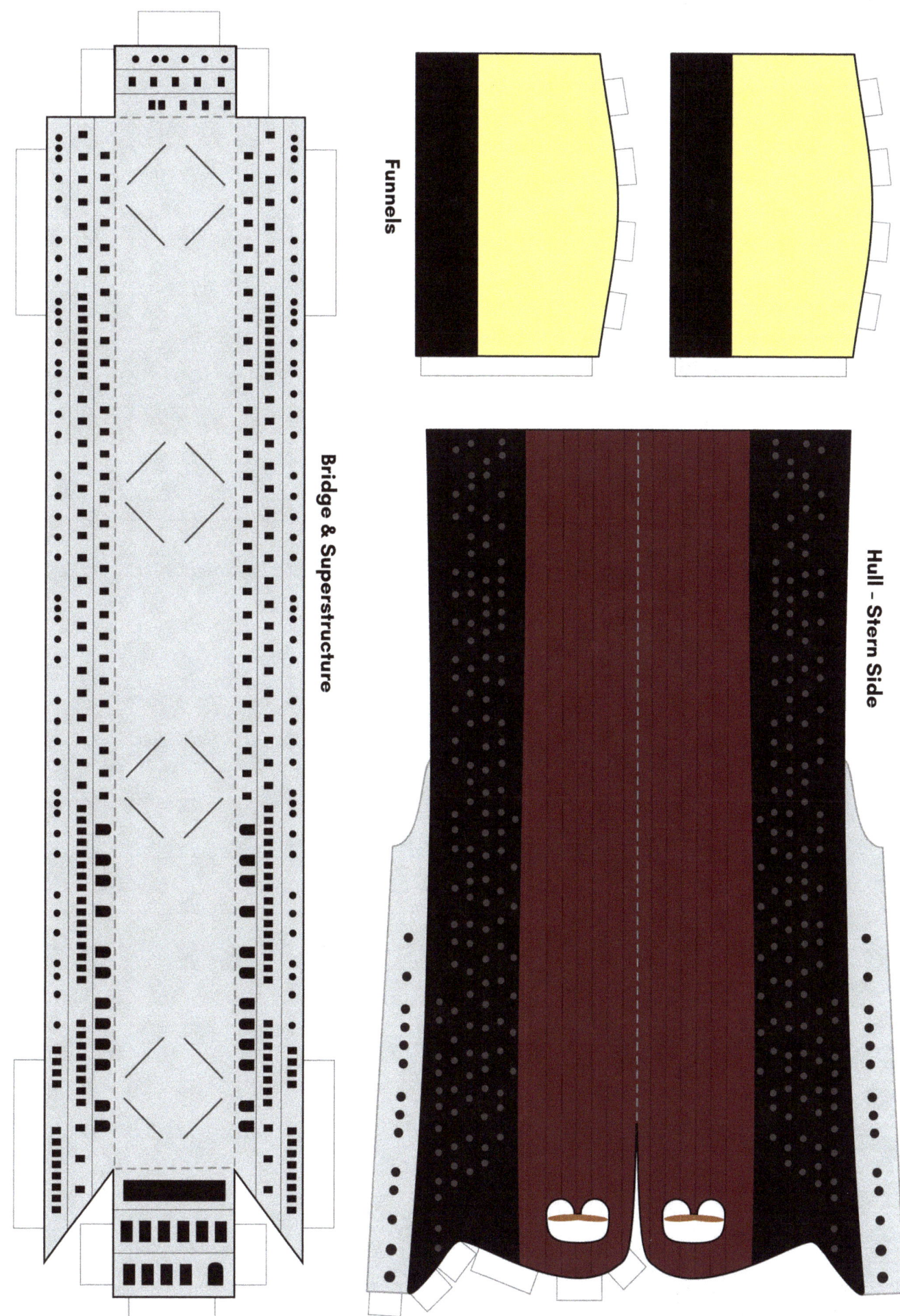

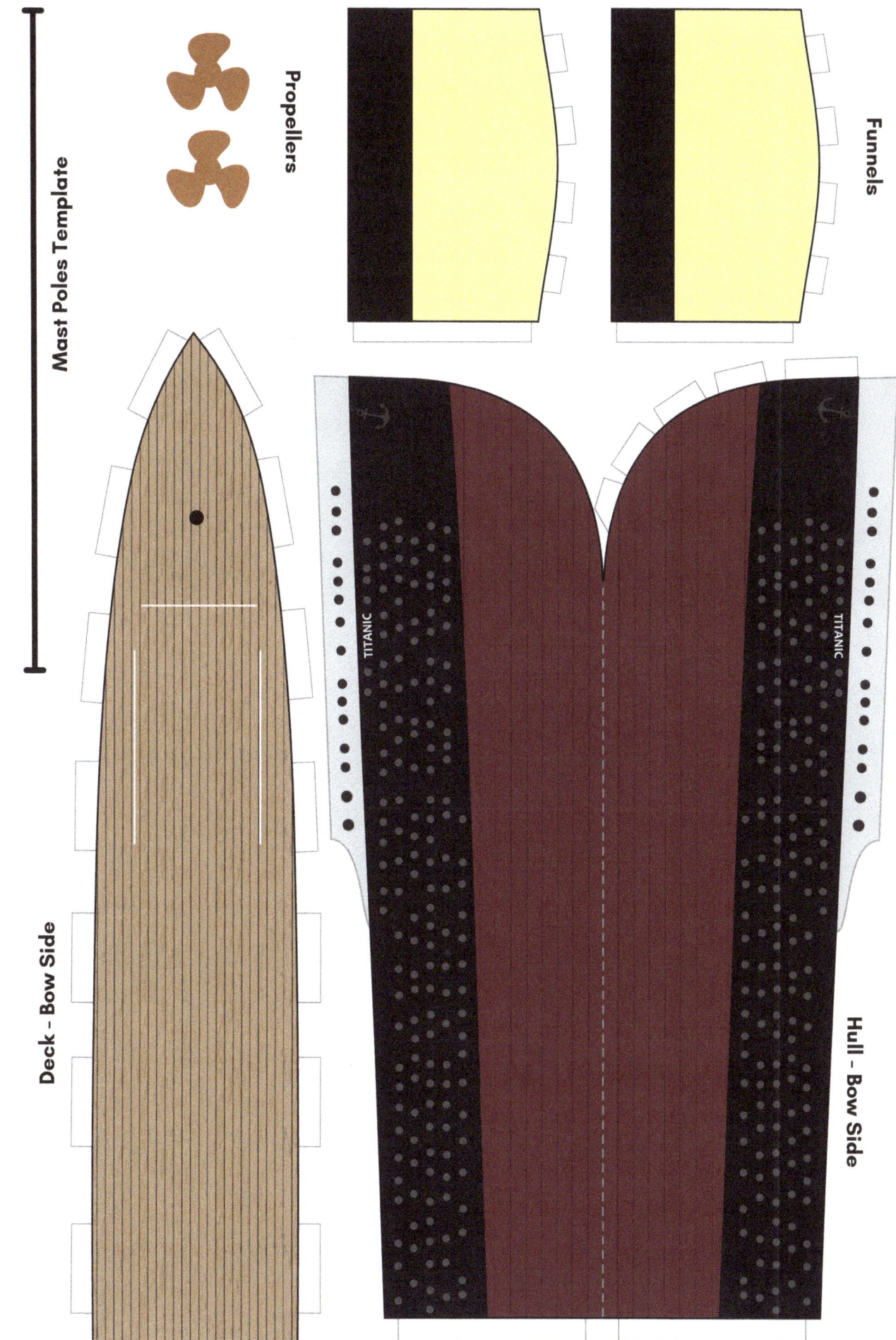

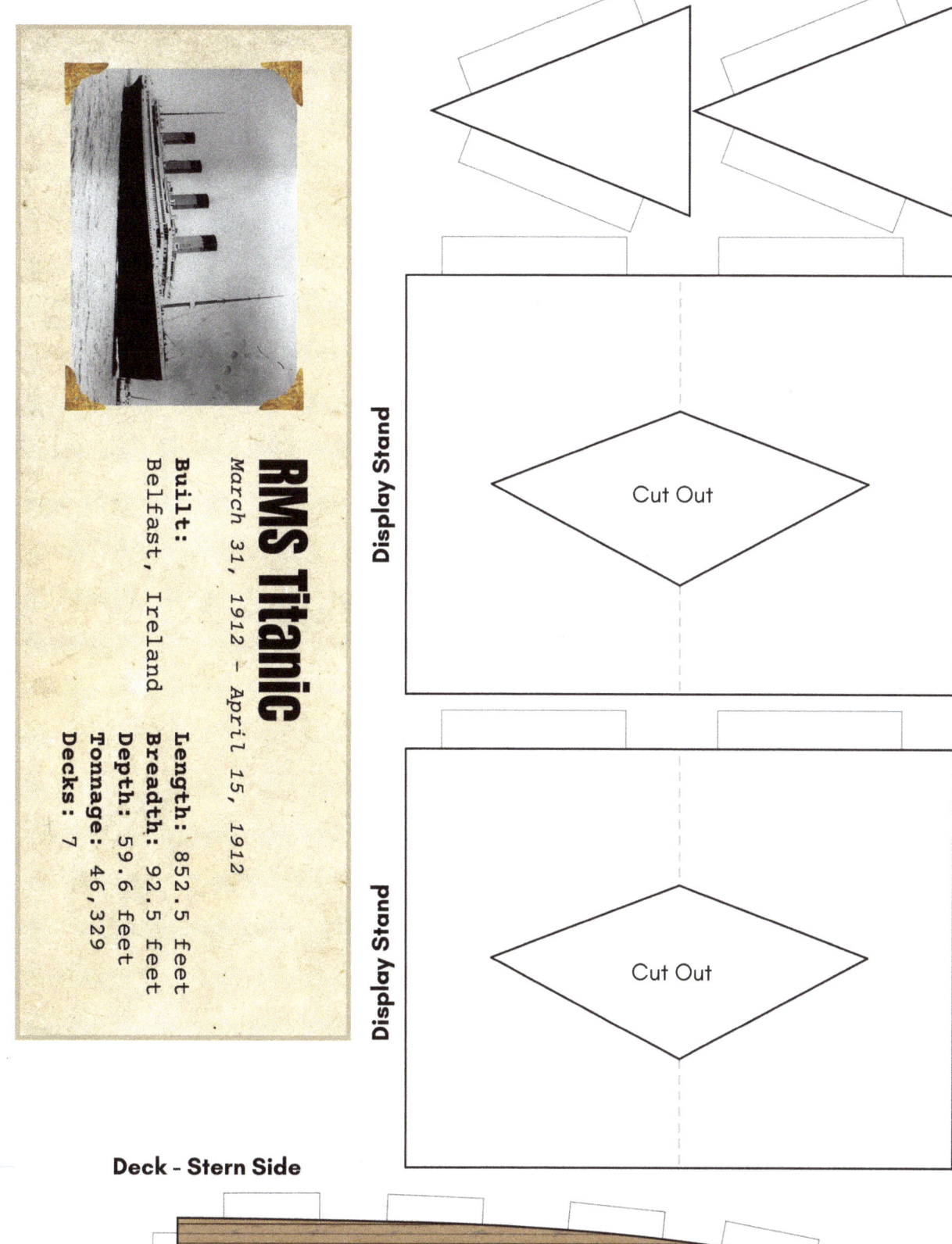

Titanic's Shipwreck Site

Cut out ship icon. Glue onto a toothpick or metal pin and identify the location of the shipwreak.

Irish Language Cards

Dia dhuit

Hello

Maidin mhaith

Good Morning

Fáilte

Welcome

Déan deifir!

Hurry up!

Irish Language Cards

Ádh mór ort
Good Luck

Le do thoil
Please

Slán

Goodbye

Go raibh maith agat

Thank you

Savy Activities

Travel the world through the interactive learning activities of **Savy Activities**; these hands-on resources provide parents, caregivers and educators practical ways to teach children about the world around them. Each book features a country, location or time period where subjects such as geography, history, vocabulary, reading, language, science, mathematics, music and art come alive by engaging auditory, visual and kinesthetic learning styles.

All activity books include geography with applicable maps, landmarks and locations. Historical events and time periods are visually represented with full color posters and flashcards, if applicable. Each book includes a set of fun-fact cards, poster and flag, if applicable. Paper models allow children to create 3D creations of major landmarks and structures. All books include a life cycle and anatomy of a plant, animal or organic compound, with flashcards and 3-part cards featuring important structures applicable to the theme.

Children learn scientific principles through active experiments and activities. Traditional customs, festivals, toys, clothing and art are also explored. Each book includes an exclusive themed mini-story featuring historical events or traditional mythology and folklore to promote vocabulary and reading. Where applicable, world languages are introduced through engaging flashcards, posters and tracing work. Each country has been meticulously researched by interviewing native persons and/or personal travel experiences to ensure the authentic culture is fully explored.

Savy Activities utilizes concepts from multiple educational methods to create unique resources allowing children a tangible and enjoyable way to explore their world. The **Savy Activities** series should not be viewed as a curriculum, but rather complimentary thematic resources to enhance traditional education. Because the individual needs and knowledge of children varies within standardized grade levels, **Savy Activities** resources have the flexibility to be used with preschool learners through early to mid-elementary years. For younger learners, adult supervision and/or assistance may be needed and activities presented in a simplified version. For older learners, resources may be paired with additional content from other materials to meet learning outcomes.

Check out our other products and resources at **www.SavyActivities.com**

www.ingramcontent.com/pod-product-compliance
Lightning Source LLC
Chambersburg PA
CBHW060745240426
43665CB00054B/2997